CLASSIC KNITS

Classic Knits

15 timeless designs to knit and keep forever

ERIKA KNIGHT
COLLECTIBLES

photography by Katya de Grunwald

POTTER
CRAFT

New York

Editorial director Jane O'Shea
Creative director Helen Lewis
Designer Claire Peters
Project editor Lisa Pendreigh
Editorial assistant Andrew Bayliss
Pattern checker Eva Yates and Sally Harding
Photographer Katya de Grunwald
Photographer's assistant Amy Gwatkin
Stylist Beth Dadswell
Hair and make-up artist Anita Keeling
Model Amy Browne at Premier Model Management
Production director Vincent Smith
Production controller Ruth Deary

Published in the United States by
Potter Craft, an imprint of the Crown
Publishing Group, a division of Random
House, Inc., New York.

www.crownpublishing.com
www.pottercraft.com

POTTER CRAFT and
CLARKSON N. POTTER
are trademarks and
POTTER and colophon are registered
trademarks of Random House, Inc.

Originally published in Great Britain by
Quadrille Publishing Limited, London.

Library of Congress Cataloging-in-Publication
Data is available.

ISBN-13: 978-0-307-34719-0
ISBN-10: 0-307-34719-2

Printed and bound in China

10 9 8 7 6 5 4 3 2 1

First Potter Craft Edition

introduction

Classic is a contemporary collection of knitted wardrobe basics. Each garment has been considered, crafted, and constructed to enhance and flatter the female form, creating highly wearable shapes that will work in myriad colorways and textures, designed to withstand the vagaries of fashion. Garments range from a quintessential round-neck cardigan to a practical v-neck tank top, an unstructured jacket to a perfect turtleneck sweater. Accessories include elegant gloves and scarf, as well as cozy socks. The range of yarns is natural, comfortable, and eminently wearable: cotton, alpaca, merino, mohair, cashmere blends, linen, and string. The garments are worked in a flattering palette of almond, stone, soft blues, subtle pinks, muted grays, and, of course, basic black to underline the timeless appeal of the designs.

the
classic
collection

the
patterns

cable scarf

materials

Any medium-weight wool yarn, such as Rowan *RYC Cashsoft Aran*
   Four 1¾ oz (50g) balls
Pair of size 7 (4.5mm) knitting needles
2 stitch holders

size

One size, approximately 42 in (106.5cm) long

gauge

19 sts and 25 rows = 4 in (10cm) over St st using size 7 (4.5mm) needles
   or whatever size necessary to obtain gauge

See pages 10–11

cable scarf

stitches

C6B (cable 6 back)
Slip next 3 sts onto cn and hold at back of work, k3, then k3 from cn.

C6F (cable 6 front)
Slip next 3 sts onto cn and hold at front of work, k3, then k3 from cn.

upward cable
(worked over 12 sts)
Row 1 (RS): K.
Row 2: P.
Row 3: C6B, C6F.
Row 4: P.
Row 5: K.
Row 6: P.
Row 7: K.
Row 8: P.

downward cable
(worked over 12 sts)
Row 1 (RS): K.
Row 2: P.
Row 3: C6F, C6B.
Row 4: P.
Row 5: K.
Row 6: P.
Row 7: K.
Row 8: P.

To make scarf

Using size 7 (4.5mm) needles, cast on 50 sts.

Rib row 1 (RS): *K2, p1, rep from * to last 2 sts, k2.

Rib row 2: P2, *k1, p2, rep from * to end.

Rep last 2 rows twice.

Beg upward cable patt as foll:

Next row (RS): [K1, p1] 3 times, k13, p1, work row 1 of upward cable over next 12 sts, [p1, k1] 9 times.

Next row: [P1, k1] 9 times, work row 2 of upward cable over next 12 sts, k1, p13, [k1, p1] 3 times.

Keeping rib and upward cable pattern correct as set, cont in patt **and at the same time** working dec 3 sts in from edge, dec 1 st by working p2tog at end of next row and then at same edge on every foll 6th row until 38 sts rem, ending with WS facing for next row.

Next row (WS): [P1, k1] 3 times, p26, [k1, p1] 3 times.

Next row (RS): [K1, p1] 3 times, k26, [p1, k1] 3 times.

Cont in St st as now set, with 6-st rib border at each edge, until scarf measures 31 in (78.5cm) from cast-on edge, ending with RS facing for next row.

Beg shaping slit in scarf as foll:

Next row (RS): Rib 6, k12, p1, k2tog, k11, rib 6.

Next row: Rib 6, p12, then turn, leaving rem sts on a holder.

Work 18 rows in patt as set on these 18 sts.

Break off yarn and leave sts on a holder.

With WS facing, rejoin yarn to rem 19 sts left on first holder and work as foll:

Next row (WS): K1, work row 2 of downward cable over next 12 sts, rib 6.

Next row: Rib 3, inc 1 in next st, rib 2, work row 3 of downward cable over next 12 sts, p1.

Keeping downward cable and rib sts correct as set, work 17 rows **and at the same time** inc 1 st at same edge of every foll 6th row.

Both sides of slit have now been completed.

Next row (RS): Rib 3, inc 1 in next st, rib 5, work row 5 of downward cable over next 12 sts, p1, k into front and back of first st on holder, k next 11 sts from holder and then rib 6 from holder—*42 sts*.

Next row: Rib 6, p13, k1, p12, rib to end.

Cont as set, inc 1 st as set on same edge of every 6th row until there are 50 sts on needle.

Work 1 row (row 6 of downward cable), ending with RS facing for next row.

Work 6 rows rib as for other end of scarf.

Bind off in rib.

To finish

Weave in any loose yarn ends. Gently steam to enhance the yarn, avoiding "pressing" cable design. Pass end of scarf through slit to keep in place when worn.

casual sweater

materials

Any super-bulky-weight wool yarn, such as Debbie Bliss
Cashmerino Superchunky
8 (9, 10, 11, 12, 13) × 1¾ oz (50g) balls
Pair each of sizes 10½ (7mm) and 11 (7.5mm) knitting needles

sizes

to fit bust	32	34	36	38	40	42	in
	81	86	91	97	102	107	cm
actual bust	34	36	38	40	42	44	in
	86	91	97	102	107	112	cm
length	21	22½	23½	24½	25½	26½	in
	53	57	60	62	65	67	cm
sleeve seam	16½	16½	17	17	17½	18	in
	42	42	43	43	44.5	46	cm

gauge

12 sts and 17 rows = 4 in (10cm) over St st using size 11 (7.5mm) needles
or whatever size necessary to obtain gauge

See pages 12–13

pattern note

• After ribbing, work increases and decreases three stitches inside the edges to create a fully fashioned detail. Work the decreases through the back of loops as foll:

On a k row: K3, k2tog, k to last 5 sts, k2tog tbl, k3.

On a p row: P3, p2tog tbl, p to last 5 sts, p2tog, p3.

Back

Using size 10½ (7mm) needles, cast on 53 (58: 58: 63: 68: 68) sts.

Rib row 1 (RS): *K3, p2, rep from * to last 3 sts, k3.

Rib row 2: *P3, k2, rep from * to last 3 sts, p3.

Rep last 2 rows until back measures 2¼ (2¼: 2¼: 2¼: 3¼: 3¼)in (5.5: 5.5: 5.5: 5.5: 8.5: 8.5)cm, ending with WS facing for next row.

Next row (WS): Rib as set, inc 1 st at end of row on 1st and 6th sizes, dec 1 st at end of row on 2nd size, inc 1 st at each end of row on 3rd size, and dec 1 st at each end of row on 5th size—*54 (57: 60: 63: 66: 69) sts.*

Change to size 11 (7.5mm) needles and beg with a K row, work in St st, dec 1 st at each end of 5th row and every foll 6th row until 46 (49: 52: 55: 58: 61) sts rem.

Cont in St st throughout, work even for 11 (13: 13: 13: 15: 15) rows, ending with RS facing for next row. Inc 1 st at each end of next row

and every foll 8th row until there are 52 (55: 58: 61: 64: 67) sts.

Work even until back measures 14 (15: 15½: 16: 16½: 17)in (35: 38: 39.5: 40.5: 42: 43)cm from cast-on edge, ending with RS facing for next row.

Shape armholes

Bind off 3sts at beg of next 2 rows—*46 (49: 52: 55: 58: 61) sts.*

Dec 1 st at each end of next and foll 3 (3: 3: 3: 4: 5) alt rows—*38 (41: 44: 47: 48: 49) sts.*

Work even until armhole measures 7 (7½: 8: 8½: 9: 9½)in (18: 19: 20.5: 21.5: 23: 24)cm, ending with RS facing for next row.

Shape shoulders and neck

Next row (RS): Bind off 4 (4: 4: 6: 6: 6) sts, work until there are 7 (8: 9: 8: 9: 9) sts on right-hand needle, then turn, leaving rem sts unworked.

Bind off 3 sts at beg of next row.

Bind off rem 4 (5: 6: 5: 6: 6) sts.

With RS facing, rejoin yarn to rem sts and bind off center 16 (17: 18:

19: 18: 19) sts, then complete to match first side, reversing all shaping.

Front

Work as for back until there are 10 (10: 10: 10: 12: 12) rows fewer worked than back to start of shoulder shaping, ending with RS facing for next row.

Shape neck

Next row (RS): K15 (16: 17: 19: 19: 19), then turn, leaving rem sts on a holder.

Work each side separately.

Bind off 3 sts at beg of next row—*12 (13: 14: 16: 16: 16) sts.*

Dec 1 st at neck edge on next 3 rows and then on foll 1 (1: 1: 2: 1: 1) alt rows—*8 (9: 10: 11: 12: 12) sts.*

Work even for 3 (3: 3: 1: 5: 5) rows, ending with RS facing for next row.

Shape shoulders

Bind off 4 (4: 4: 6: 6: 6) sts at beg of next row.

Work even for 1 row.

Bind off rem 4 (5: 6: 5: 6: 6) sts.

With RS facing, rejoin yarn to rem sts and bind off center 8 (9: 10: 9: 10: 11) sts, then complete to match first side, reversing all shaping.

Sleeves

Using size 10½ (7mm) needles, cast on 30 (30: 30: 35: 35: 35) sts.
Rib row 1 (RS): *K3, p2, rep from * to end.
Rib row 2: *K2, p3, rep from * to end.
Rep last 2 rows until rib measures 4 (4: 4: 4: 5: 5)in (10: 10: 10: 10: 12.5: 12.5)cm from cast-on edge, ending with WS facing for next row.
Next row (WS): Rib as set, inc 3 sts across row on 3rd size, and inc 1 st at end of row on 5th and 6th sizes—*30 (30: 33: 35: 36: 36) sts.*
Change to size 11 (7.5mm) needles and beg with a k row, work in St st, inc 1 st at each end of 5th row and every foll 8th row until there are 40 (42: 45: 45: 46: 48) sts.
Cont in St st throughout, work even until sleeve measures 16½ (16½: 17: 17: 17½: 18)in (42: 42: 43: 43: 44.5: 46)cm from cast-on edge, ending with RS facing for next row.

Shape cap

Bind off 3 (3: 3: 3: 3: 3) sts at beg of next 2 rows.
Dec 1 st at each end of next row and every foll alt row until 26 (28: 29: 29: 30: 32) sts rem.
Dec 1 st at each end of foll 4th row—*24 (26: 27: 27: 28: 30) sts.*
Work even for 3 rows.
Dec 1 st at each end of next row and foll alt row, then on foll 3 rows.
Bind off 3 sts at beg of next 2 rows.
Bind off rem 10 (12: 13: 13: 14: 15) sts.

Collar

Sew right shoulder seam.
Using size 10½ (7mm) needles and with RS facing, pick up and k 14 (14: 13: 13: 16: 16) sts down left side of front neck, 8 (9: 10: 9: 10: 11) sts across center front, 14 (14: 13: 13: 16: 16) sts up right side of front neck, and 22 (23: 24: 25: 24: 25) sts across back neck—*58 (60: 60: 60: 66: 68) sts.*

1st and 6th sizes only
Next row: K2, p3, k into front and back of next st, [p3, k2] twice, p3, k into front and back of next st, p3, *k2, p3, rep from * to end—*60 (—: —: —: —: 70) sts.*

5th size only
Next row: K2tog, k1, *p3, k2, rep from * to last 3 sts, p3— — (—: —: —: 65: —) sts.*

All sizes
Next row: *K3, p2, rep from * to end.
Work 4 in (10cm) in rib as set.
Bind off in rib.

To finish

Weave in any loose yarn ends.
Lay work out flat and gently steam to enhance the yarn.
Sew collar and shoulder seam.
Sew sleeve heads into armholes.
Sew side and sleeve seams.

messenger bag

materials

Any medium natural colored kitchen twine (from hardware or stationery stores)
  Nine 88 yd (80m) balls
Pair of size 7 (4.5mm) knitting needles
Piece of leather, approximately 3 in (7.5cm) by 5 in (13cm), for handle
2 large buttons, 2 medium-size buttons, and 2 large snaps

size

One size, approximately 13 in (33cm) by 10½ in (26.5cm)

gauge

14 sts and 24 rows = 4 in (10cm) over seed st using size 7 (4.5mm) needles
  or whatever size necessary to obtain gauge

Back
Using 4.5mm needles, cast on 47 sts.
Row 1: K1, *p1, k1, rep from * to end.
Rep last row to form seed st and
keeping seed st patt correct as set
throughout, work 64 rows, dec 1 st at
each end of rows 21 and 42—*43 sts.***
Mark each end of last row to mark
fold line of front flap.
Work 55 rows, inc 1 st at each end
of row 21—*45 sts.*
Bind off in seed st.

Front
Work as for back to **.
Bind off in seed st.

Straps (make 2)
Using size 7 (4.5mm) needles, cast
on 17 sts.
Working in seed st as for back and
keeping patt correct as set
throughout, work 39 rows.
Mark each end of last row to mark
bottom corner of bag.
Dec 1 st at each end of every foll
16th row until 11 sts rem.
Work even for 16 rows.
Mark each end of last row to mark
corner of bag.
Work 113 rows, dec 1 st at each
end of row 20—*9 sts.*
Bind off in seed st.

To finish
Weave in any loose yarn ends.
Working all seams as external
seams, sew cast-on edges of straps
together to form center bottom of
gusset of bag.
Sew front and back to strap
between markers, allowing flap
to fold to front.
Sew large buttons to front flap
and snaps underneath.
Sew one medium-size button to
each strap end.
Trim leather to width of strap
and cut a buttonhole at each end.
Button leather strip onto straps.

See pages 14–15

wraparound jacket

materials

Any super-bulky-weight wool yarn, such as Rowan *Spray*
  10 (11, 12) × 3½ oz (100g) balls
Pair of size 15 (10mm) knitting needles

sizes

to fit bust				
to fit bust	32–34	36–38	40–42	in
	81–86	91–97	102–107	cm
actual bust	42	46	50	in
	106	117	127	cm
length	25	27	29	in
	63.5	68.5	73.5	cm
sleeve seam	18	18½	19	in
	46	47	48	cm

gauge

9 sts and 12 rows = 4 in (10cm) over St st using size 15 (10mm) needles
  or whatever size necessary to obtain gauge

See pages 16–17

pattern notes

- As the row-end edges of the fronts form the actual finished edge of the garment, it is important that all new balls of yarn are joined in at the side seam or the armhole edges of rows.
- Work increases and decreases three stitches inside the edges to create a fully fashioned detail. Work the decreases through the back of loops as foll:
  On a k row: K3, k2tog, k to last 5 sts, k2tog tbl, k3.
  On a p row: P3, p2tog tbl, p to last 5 sts, p2tog, p3.

Back

Using size 15 (10mm) needles, cast on 48 (52: 56) sts.

Rib row 1 (RS): *K1, p1, rep from * to end.

Rep last row once.

Beg with a k row, work in St st until back measures 16½ (17½: 18½)in (42: 44.5: 47)cm from cast-on edge, ending with RS facing for next row.

Shape armhole

Bind off 3 sts at beg of next 2 rows—*42 (46: 50) sts.*

Dec 1 st at each end of next 3 rows—*36 (40: 44) sts.*

Work even until armhole measures 8½ (9½: 10½)in (21.5: 24: 26.5)cm, ending with RS facing for next row.

Shape shoulders

Bind off 4 (5: 5) sts at beg of next 2 rows and 5 (5: 6) sts at beg of foll 2 rows—*18 (20: 22) sts.*

Work 6 in (15cm) in k1, p1 rib.

Bind off in rib.

Right front

Using size 15 (10mm) needles, cast on 40 (44: 48) sts.

Work 2 rows in rib as for back.

Next row (RS): [K1, p1] 9 times, k to end.

Next row: P to last 18 sts, [k1, p1] 9 times.

Rep last 2 rows until front measures 13½ (14½: 15½)in (34.5: 37: 39.5)cm from cast-on edge, ending

with RS facing for next row.

Add 2 extra sts into rib section as foll:

Next row (RS): [K1, p1] 10 times, k to end.

Cont to add 2 extra sts into rib section on every foll 8th row until 26 (28: 30) sts are being ribbed **and at the same time** when work measures 16½ (17½: 18½)in (42: 44.5: 47)cm from cast-on edge, ending with WS facing for next row, shape armhole as foll:

Shape armhole

Bind off 3 sts at beg of row—*37 (41: 45) sts.*

Dec 1 st at armhole edge of next 3 rows—*34 (38: 42) sts.*

Work even until armhole measures 8½ (9½: 10½)in (21.5: 24: 26.5)cm, ending with WS facing for next row.

Shape shoulder
Bind off 4 (5: 5) sts at beg of next row and 5 (5: 6) sts at beg of foll alt row—*25 (28: 31) sts.*
Work 6 in (15cm) in k1, p1 rib.
Bind off in rib.

Left front
Using size 15 (10mm) needles, cast on 40 (44: 48) sts.
Work 2 rows in rib as for back.
Next row (RS): K to last 17 sts, [p1, k1] 8 times, p1.
Next row: K1, [p1, k1] 8 times, p to end.

Rep last 2 rows until front measures 13½ (14½: 15½)in (34.5: 37: 39.5)cm from cast-on edge, ending with RS facing for next row.
Add 2 extra sts into rib section as foll:
Next row: K to last 19 sts, [p1, k1] 9 times, p1.
Complete to match right front, reversing all shaping, but increasing rib section to only 25 (27: 29) sts.

Sleeves (make 2)
Cast on 30 (30: 32) sts.
Work 4 in (10cm) in k1, p1 rib.
Beg with a k, work in St st, inc 1 st at each end of 7th row and every foll 8th row until there are

38 (42: 46) sts.
Cont in St st throughout, work even until sleeve measures 18 (18½: 19½)in (46: 47: 48)cm from cast-on edge, ending with RS facing for next row.

Shape cap
Bind off 3 sts at beg of next 2 rows—*32 (36: 40) sts.*
Dec 1 st at each end next row and foll 3 alt rows—*24 (28: 32) sts.*
Work even for 1 row. Bind off.

To finish
Weave in any loose yarn ends.
Gently steam to enhance the yarn.
Sew shoulder and collar seams. Sew sleeve heads to armholes. Sew side and sleeve seams.

military cardigan

materials

Any lightweight wool yarn, such as Rowan *Tapestry*
    8 (9, 9, 10, 11, 11) × 1¾ oz (50g) balls
Pair each of sizes 5 (3.75mm) and 6 (4mm) knitting needles
13 buttons
9 snaps

sizes

to fit bust	32	34	36	38	40	42	in
	81	86	91	97	102	107	cm
actual bust	34	36	38	40½	42½	45	in
	86	92	97	103	108	114	cm
length	20	21	22	23	24	24	in
	51	53	56	58.5	61	61	cm
sleeve seam	18	18	19	19	19	19½	in
	46	46	48.5	48.5	48.5	49.5	cm

gauge

24 sts and 32 rows = 4 in (10cm) over St st using size 6 (4mm) needles
    or whatever size necessary to obtain gauge

pattern note

• Work increases and decreases at armholes, neck, and on pocket
flaps three stitches inside the edges to create a fully fashioned
detail. Work the decreases through the back of loops as foll:
On a k row: K3, k2tog, k to last 5 sts, k2tog tbl, k3.
On a p row: P3, p2tog tbl, p to last 5 sts, p2tog, p3.

See pages 18–19

military cardigan

Back

Using size 5 (3.75mm) needles, cast on 105 (110: 115: 120: 125: 135) sts.

Rib row 1 (RS): *K3, p2, rep from * to end.

Rib row 2: *K2, p3, rep from * to end.

Rep last 2 rows until back measures 2¾ in (7cm), ending with WS facing for next row.

Next row (WS): Rib as set, dec 1 st at each end of row on 1st and 6th sizes, dec 1 st at end of row on 2nd size, inc 1 st at end of row on 4th size, and inc 1 st at each end of row on 5th size—*103 (109: 115: 121: 127: 133) sts.*

Change to size 6 (4mm) needles and St st and work even until back measures 13 (13½: 14: 15: 15½: 15)in (32: 33: 34: 36: 37: 37)cm, ending with RS facing for next row.

Shape armholes

Bind off 6 sts at beg of next 2 rows, then dec 1 st at each end of foll 5 rows and then foll 4 alt rows—*73 (79: 85: 91: 97: 103) sts.*

Work even until armhole measures 7 (7½: 8: 8: 8½: 9)in (17.5: 19: 20: 20: 21.5: 23)cm, ending with RS facing for next row.

Shape shoulder and neck

Bind off 6 (6: 7: 8: 8: 9) sts at beg of next 2 rows.

Next row (RS): Bind off 5 (6: 7: 8: 9: 10) sts, work until there are

9 (11: 11: 12: 13: 14) sts on right needle, turn.

Bind off 4 sts at beg of next row.

Bind off rem 5 (7: 7: 8: 9: 10) sts.

With RS facing, rejoin yarn to rem sts and bind off center 33 (33: 35: 35: 37: 37) sts, then k to end.

Complete to match first side, reversing all shaping.

Right front

Using size 5 (3.75mm) needles, cast on 60 (60: 65: 70: 70: 75) sts.

Rib row 1 (RS): [K1, p1] 5 times, *k3, p2, rep from * to end.

Rib row 2: *K2, p3, rep from * to last 10 sts, [k1, p1] 5 times.

Rep last 2 rows until front measures 2¾ in (7cm), ending with WS facing for next row.

Next row (WS): Rib as set, dec 1 st at beg of row on 1st and 6th sizes, inc 1 st at beg and middle of row on 2nd size, dec 1 st at beg and middle of row on 4th size, and inc 1 st at beg of row on 5th size—*59 (62: 65: 68: 71: 74) sts.*

Change to size 6 (4mm) needles and keeping 10 k1, p1 rib sts as set for button band, cont in St st until front measures same as back to armhole, ending with WS facing for next row.

Shape armhole

Bind off 6 sts at beg of next row, then dec 1 st at armhole edge of foll 5 rows and every foll alt row 4

times—*44 (47: 50: 53: 56: 59) sts.*

Work even until front measures 2 (2: 2: 2: 2¼: 2¼)in (5: 5: 5: 5: 5.5: 5.5)cm less than back to shoulder, ending with RS facing for next row.

Shape neck

Next row (RS): Rib first 10 sts and leave on a holder, bind off next 7 (7: 9: 9: 9: 9) sts, k to end.

Bind off 4 sts at beg of next alt row, then dec 1 st at neck edge on foll 3 rows and then on every foll alt row until there are 16 (19: 21: 24: 26: 29) sts.

Work even until front measures same as back to shoulder, ending with WS facing for next row.

Bind off 6 (6: 7: 8: 8: 9) sts at beg of next row and 5 (6: 7: 8: 9: 10) sts at beg of foll alt row.

Work even for 1 row.

Bind off rem 5 (7: 7: 8: 9: 10) sts.

Left front

Using size 5 (3.75mm) needles, cast on 60 (60: 65: 70: 70: 75) sts.

Row 1 (RS): *K3, p2, rep from * to last 10 sts, [k1, p1] 5 times.

Row 2: [K1, p1] 5 times, *k2, p3, rep from * to end.

Rep last 2 rows until front measures 2¾ in (7cm), ending with WS facing for next row.

Next row (WS): Rib as set, dec 1 st at end of row on 1st and 6th sizes, inc 1 st at middle and end of row on 2nd size, dec 1 st at middle

of and end of row on 4th size, and inc 1 st at end of row on 5th size—*59 (62: 65: 68: 71: 74) sts.*
Change to size 6 (4mm) needles and keeping 10 k1, p1 rib sts as set for button band, cont in St st and complete as for right front, reversing all shaping.

Sleeve (make 2)

Using size 5 (3.75mm) needles, cast on 55 (55: 55: 60: 60: 60) sts.
Row 1 (RS): *K3, p2, rep from * to end.
Row 2: *K2, p3, rep from * to end.
Rep last 2 rows until sleeve measures 5½ in (14cm) ending with RS facing for next row.
Change to size 6 (4mm) needles and beg with a k row, work in St st, inc 1 st at each end of 7th row and every foll 8th row until there are 77 (79: 79: 82: 84: 88) sts.
Work even until sleeve measures 18 (18: 19: 19: 19: 19½)in (46: 46: 48.5: 48.5: 49.5)cm from cast-on edge, ending with RS facing for next row.

Shape cap

Bind off 5 sts at beg of next 2 rows, then dec 1 st at each end of foll 5 rows and every foll alt row until 25 (27: 27: 30: 32: 36) sts rem.
Dec 1 st at each end of next 5 rows.
Bind off rem 15 (17: 17: 20: 22: 26) sts.

Pockets (make 2)

Using size 6 (4mm) needles, cast on 20 (20: 20: 23: 23: 23) sts.
Row 1 (RS): P1, k1, p1, k to last 3 sts, p1, k1, p1.
Row 2: K1, p1, k1, p to last 3 sts, k1, p1, k1.
Row 3: P1, k1, p1, M1, k to last 3 sts, M1, p1, k1, p1.
Row 4: K1, p1, k1, p to last 3 sts, k1, p1, k1.
Rep last 2 rows twice—*26 (26: 26: 29: 29: 29) sts.*
Keeping rib patt correct as set, work even until pocket measures 4½ (4½: 4½: 5: 5: 5)in (11.5: 11.5: 11.5: 13: 13: 13)cm from cast-on edge.
Bind off.

Pocket tops (make 2)

Using size 6 (4mm) needles, cast on 28 (28: 28: 31: 31: 31) sts.
Rep rows 1 and 2 of pocket 3 times.
Keeping patt correct as set, dec 1 st at each end of every row (inside rib sts) until 8 sts rem, ending with RS facing for next row.
Next row: P1, k1, k2tog, k2tog tbl, k1, p1.
Next row: K1, p2tog tbl, p2tog, k1—*4 sts.*
Next row: K2tog, k2tog tbl—*2 sts.*
Next row: P2tog and fasten off.

Epaulettes for shoulders (make 2)

Using size 5 (3.75mm) needles, cast on 10 sts.
Work 4 in (10cm) in k1, p1 rib.
Bind off in rib.

To finish

Weave in any loose yarn ends.
Gently steam with care.
Sew both shoulder seams.

Collar

Using size 5 (3.75mm) needles and with RS facing, rib 10 sts from holder as set, pick up and k 25 (25: 27: 27: 29: 29) sts along right front neck, 42 (42: 43: 43: 44: 44) sts across center back, 25 (25: 27: 27: 29: 29) sts along left front neck, and rib 10 sts from holder—*112 (112: 117: 117: 123: 123) sts.*
Next row (WS): Rib 10 sts, *k2, p3, rep from * to last 12 sts, k2, rib 10 sts.
Work in rib patt as set until collar measures 3¼ in (8cm).
Bind off in rib.
Sew sleeve heads to armholes.
Sew side and sleeve seams.
Sew on pockets above ribbing, then sew on flaps.
Sew cast-on edge of epaulettes to armhole seam.
Sew one button to each pocket flap and end of each epaulette, securing epaulettes in place at same time.
Sew rem buttons evenly spaced along front bands and collar.
Sew on snaps under buttons on front band.

tank top

materials

Any super-bulky-weight wool yarn, such as Rowan *Big Wool*
   3 (3, 3, 4, 4, 5) × 3 ½ oz (100g) balls
Pair each of sizes 15 (10mm) and 17 (12mm) knitting needles

sizes

to fit bust	32	34	36	38	40	42	in
	81	86	91	97	102	107	cm
actual bust	32	34	36	38	40	42	in
	81	86	91	97	102	107	cm
length	17 ½	18 ½	19 ½	20 ½	21 ½	22 ½	in
	44.5	47	49.5	52	54	57	cm

gauge

18 sts and 12 rows = 4 in (10cm) over St st using size 17 (12mm) needles
   to whatever size necessary to obtain gauge

See pages 20–21

tank top

pattern note

• To create a fully fashioned detail, work increases and decreases two or three stitches inside the edges as instructed.

Back

Using size 15 (10mm) needles, cast on 33 (33: 36: 39: 39: 42) sts.

Rib row 1 (RS): *K2, p1, rep from * to end.

Rib row 2: *K1, p2, rep from * to end.

Rep last 2 rows until back measures 6 (6½: 6½: 7: 7: 7½)in (15: 17: 17: 18: 18: 19)cm from cast-on edge, ending with WS facing for next row.

Next row (WS): Rib as set, dec 1 st at beg of row on 1st and 4th sizes, and inc 1 st at beg of row on 2nd and 5th sizes—*32 (34: 36: 38: 40: 42) sts.***

Change to size 17 (12mm) needles and beg with a k row, work in St st until back measures 11 (11½: 12: 12½: 13: 13½)in (27.5: 29: 30.5: 32: 32: 34)cm from cast-on edge, ending with RS facing for next row.

Shape armhole

Cont in St st throughout, bind off 2 sts at beg of next 2 rows—*28 (30: 32: 34: 36: 38) sts.*

Next row (RS): K2, k2tog, k to last 4 sts, k2tog tbl, k2.

Next row: P.

Rep last 2 rows once more—*24 (26: 28: 30: 32: 34) sts.*

Work even until armhole measures

6½ (7: 7½: 8: 8½: 9)in (17: 18: 19: 20: 22: 23)cm, ending with RS facing for next row.

Shape shoulders and neck

Next row (RS): Bind off 4 (4: 4: 4: 5: 5) sts, k until there are 4 (4: 5: 5: 5: 5) sts on right-hand needle, then turn.

Bind off rem 4 (4: 5: 5: 5: 5) sts.

With RS facing, rejoin yarn to rem sts and bind off center 8 (10: 10: 12: 12: 14) sts, then k to end.

Complete to match first side, reversing all shaping.

Front

Work as for back to **.

Change to size 17 (12mm) needles and beg with a k row, work 4 (4: 4: 6: 6: 6) rows in St st.

Next row (RS): K16 (17: 18: 19: 20: 21), then turn, leaving rem sts on a holder.

Shape neck

Next row (WS): K1, p1, k1, p to end.

Next row: K to last 3 sts, p1, k1, p1.

Next row: K1, p1, k1, p to end. Rep last 2 rows once more.

Next row (dec row) (RS): K to last 5 sts, k2tog tbl, p1, k1, p1.

Cont in St st with 3-st rib border, dec 1 st inside 3-st rib border as set on every foll 4th row **and at the same time** when front same as back to armhole, shape armhole as for back.

Cont dec at neck edge on every 4th row until 8 (8: 9: 9: 10: 10) sts rem. Work even until armhole measures same as back to shoulder, ending with RS facing for next row.

Shape shoulder

Bind off 4 (4: 4: 4: 5: 5) sts at beg of next row.

Bind off rem 4 (4: 5: 5: 5: 5) sts. With RS facing, rejoin yarn to rem

sts and complete to match first side, reversing all shaping.

To finish

Weave in any loose yarn ends. Lay work out flat and gently steam. Sew shoulder seams with a flat seam. Sew side seams.

bardot sweater

materials

Any super-bulky-weight wool yarn, such as Rowan *Little Big Wool*
  11 (12, 12, 13, 14, 14) × 100g balls
Pair each of sizes 13 (9mm) and 15 (10mm) knitting needles

sizes

to fit bust	32	34	36	38	40	42	in
	81	86	91	97	102	107	cm
actual bust	36	39	42	45	48	50	in
	91.5	99	107	114.5	122	127	cm
length	18½	19½	20½	21½	22½	23½	in
	47	49.5	52	54	57	59.5	cm
sleeve seam	17½	17½	18½	18½	19½	19½	in
	44.5	44.5	47	47	49.5	49.5	cm

gauge

14 sts and 14 rows = 4 in (10cm) over rib using size 15 (10mm) needles
  or whatever size necessary to obtain gauge

See pages 22–23

bardot sweater

pattern note

• To create a fully fashioned detail, work decreases two stitches in from edge if desired.

Back

Using size 13 (9mm) needles, cast on 63 (68: 73: 78: 83: 88) sts.
Row 1 (RS): *K3, p2, rep from * to last 3 sts, k3.
Row 2: *P3, k2, rep from * to last 3 sts, p3.
Rep last 2 rows 3 times more.
Change to size 15 (10mm) needles and cont in rib as set until back measures 12 (12½: 13: 13½: 14: 14½)in (30.5: 32: 33: 34.5: 36: 37)cm from cast-on edge, ending with RS facing for next row.
Shape raglan armhole
Keeping rib patt correct as set throughout, bind off 3 sts at beg of next 2 rows—*57 (62: 67: 72:*

77: 82) sts.
Dec 1 st at each end of next 5 rows, then on foll alt row—*45 (50: 55: 60: 65: 70) sts.*
Work even until back measures 18½ (19½: 20½: 21½: 22½: 23½)in (47: 49.5: 52: 54: 57: 59.5)cm from cast-on edge, ending with RS facing for next row.
Bind off in rib.

Front

Work as for back until 4 (4: 4: 6: 6: 6) rows fewer have been worked before bind-off.
Next row (RS): Work 14 (16: 18: 20: 22: 24) sts, then turn, leaving rem sts on a holder.

Bind off 2 sts at beg of next row and foll alt row—*10 (12: 14: 16: 18: 20) sts.*
Work even for 0 (0: 0: 2: 2: 2) rows.
Bind off in rib.
With RS facing, rejoin yarn to rem sts and bind off center 17 (18: 19: 20: 21: 22) sts, then work to end.
Complete to match first side, reversing all shaping.

Sleeves (make 2)

Using size 13 (9mm) needles, cast on 33 (33: 38: 38: 43: 43) sts.
Work 8 rows in rib as for back.
Change to size 15 (10mm) needles and keeping rib correct as set throughout, inc 1 st at each end of

next row and every foll 12th row until there are 43 (43: 48: 48: 53: 53) sts, work extra sts into rib. Work even until sleeve measures 17½ (17½: 18½: 18½: 19½: 19½)in (44.5: 44.5: 47: 47: 49.5: 49.5)cm from cast-on edge, ending with RS facing for next row.

Shape raglan armhole
Bind off 3 sts at beg of next 2 rows—*37 (37: 42: 42: 47: 47) sts.*
Dec 1 st at each end of next 2 rows, then on next and foll 3 (3: 4: 4: 4: 4) alt rows, then on foll 4th row 2 (2: 2: 2: 3: 3) times—*21 (21: 24: 24: 27: 27) sts.*
Work even for 3 (3: 5: 7: 7: 9) rows.
Bind off in rib.

To finish
Sew both front and right back raglan seams.

Collar
Using size 13 (9mm) needles and RS facing, pick up and k 19 (19: 22: 22: 25: 25) sts across top of left sleeve, 14 (14: 15: 15: 16: 16) sts down left front neck, 17 (18: 19: 20: 21: 22) sts across center front neck, 14 (14: 15: 15: 16: 16) sts up right front neck, 19 (19: 22: 22: 25: 25) sts across top of right sleeve, and 44 (48: 54: 58: 64: 68) sts across back neck—*127 (132: 147: 152: 167: 172) sts.*
Row 1: *K3, p2, rep from * to last 2 sts, k2.

Row 2: P2, *k2, p3, rep from * to end.
Rep last 2 rows until collar measures 6 in (15cm), then change to size 15 (10mm) needles and work 6 in (15cm) more.
Bind off in rib.
Sew raglan and collar seam, reversing seam for last 6 in (15cm) of collar.
Sew sleeve and side seams.

kelly cardigan

materials

Any fine-weight mohair yarn, such as Rowan *Kidsilk Haze*
    6 (6, 8, 8, 10, 10) × ¾ oz (25g) balls
Pair each of sizes 3 (3mm) and 5 (3.75mm) knitting needles
9 snaps

sizes

to fit bust	32	34	36	38	40	42	in
	81	86	91	97	102	107	cm
actual bust	34	36	38	40½	42½	45	in
	86	92	97	103	108	114	cm
length	18½	19	19½	19½	20	20½	in
	47	48	49	50	51	52	cm
sleeve seam	14	14	14½	14½	14½	15	in
	36	36	37	37	37	38	cm

gauge

22 sts and 30 rows = 4 in (10cm) over St st using size 5 (3.75mm)
    needles or whatever size necessary to obtain gauge and two
    strands of yarn together

pattern notes

• Remember to use two strands of the yarn together throughout.
• To create a fully fashioned detail, work increases and decreases
  three sts inside the edges as instructed.
• Work the front k1, p1 rib buttonbands integrally with each front
  to give a neater finish and to avoid having to sew it on.

See pages 24–25

kelly cardigan

Back

Using size 3 (3mm) needles and two strands of yarn tog, cast on 87 (95: 101: 107: 113: 119) sts.

Rib row 1 (RS): *P1, k1, rep from * to last st, p1.

Rib row 2: *K1, p1, rep from * to last st, k1

Rep last 2 rows until back measures 5cm from cast-on edge, ending with RS facing for next row.

Change to size 5 (3.75mm) needles.

Next row (RS): K3, M1, k to last 3 sts, M1, k3.

Cont in St st throughout, inc 1 st in same way at each end of every foll 20th row until there are 95 (101: 107: 113: 119: 125) sts.

Work even until back measures 11½ (12: 12: 12: 12: 12½)in (29: 30: 30: 31: 31: 32)cm from cast-on edge, ending with RS facing for next row.

Shape armholes

Bind off 4 (5: 5: 6: 6: 7) sts at beg of next 2 rows and 3 sts at beg of foll 2 rows—*81 (85: 91: 95: 101: 105) sts.*

Next row (RS): K3, k2tog, k to last 5 sts, k2tog tbl, k3.

Next row: P3, p2tog tbl, p to last 5 sts, p2tog tbl, p3.

Dec 1 st in same way at each end of next 1 (1: 3: 3: 5: 5) rows and then on foll 0 (1: 1: 2: 2: 3) alt rows and then on foll 4th row—*73 (75: 77: 79: 81: 83) sts.*

Work even until armhole measures 7 (7: 7½: 7½: 8: 8)in (18: 18: 19: 19: 20: 20)cm, ending with RS facing for next row.

Shape shoulders and neck

Bind off 7 (7: 7: 7: 8: 8) sts at beg of next 2 rows—*59 (61: 63: 65: 65: 67) sts.*

Next row (RS): Bind off 7 (7: 7: 7: 8: 8) sts, k until there are 10 (10: 11: 11: 10: 11) sts on right-hand needle, then turn, leaving rem sts on a holder.

Work this side first.

Bind off 3 sts at beg of next row.

Bind off rem 7 (7: 8: 8: 7: 8) sts.

With RS facing, rejoin yarn to rem sts and bind off center 25 (27: 27: 29: 29: 29) sts, then k to end.

Complete to match first side, reversing all shaping.

Left front

Using size 3 (3mm) needles and two strands of yarn tog, cast on 53 (55: 59: 61: 65: 67) sts.

Rep 2 rib rows as for back until front measures 2 in (5cm) from cast-on edge, ending with RS facing for next row and inc 0 (1: 0: 1: 0: 1) st at end (side-seam edge) of last row—*53 (56: 59: 62: 65: 68) sts.*

Change to size 5 (3.75mm) needles.

Next row (RS): K3, M1, k to last 5 sts, p1, k1, p1, k1, p1.

Cont in St st throughout, with 5-st rib border as set, inc 1 st at side seam edge on every foll 20th row until there are 56 (59: 62: 65: 68: 71) sts.

Work even until front measures 11½ (12: 12: 12: 12: 12½)in (29: 30: 30: 31: 31: 32)cm from cast-on edge, ending with RS facing for next row.

Shape armhole

Bind off 4 (5: 5: 6: 6: 7) sts at beg of next row and 3 sts at beg of foll alt row—*49 (51: 54: 56: 59: 61) sts.*

Work even for 1 row.

Working all armhole decreases as set for back, dec 1 st at armhole edge of next 3 (3: 5: 5: 7: 7) rows, then on foll 0 (1: 1: 2: 2: 3) alt rows, then on foll 4th row—*45 (46: 47: 48: 49: 50) sts.*

Work even until 11 (11: 11: 11: 11:

13) rows fewer have been worked than for back to start of shoulder shaping, ending with WS facing for next row.

Shape neck

Next row (WS): Rib first 5 sts and leave on a holder, bind off next 8 (9: 9: 10: 10: 11) sts, p to end. Bind off 4 sts at beg of foll alt row—*28 (28: 29: 29: 30: 30) sts*. Work decreases as before, dec 1 st at neck edge on next 7 rows, then on foll 0 (0: 0: 0: 0: 1) alt rows— *21 (21: 22: 22: 23: 24) sts*. Work even for 1 row, ending with RS facing for next row.

Shape shoulder

Bind off 7 (7: 7: 7: 8: 8) sts at beg of next and foll alt row. Work even for 1 row. Bind off rem 7 (7: 8: 8: 7: 8) sts.

Right front

Work as for left front, reversing all shaping and working 1 extra row before start of armhole shaping.

Sleeves (make 2)

Using size 3 (3mm) needles and two strands of yarn tog, cast on 53 (53: 55: 57: 57: 59) sts.

Work 1¼ in (3cm) in k1, p1 rib. Change to size 5 (3.75mm) needles. Beg with a k row, work in St st throughout, inc 1 st at each end of 7th row and every foll 12th (10th: 10th: 8th: 8th: 10th) row until there are 69 (67: 67: 69: 61: 79) sts.

2nd, 3rd, 4th, and 5th sizes only

Inc 1 st at each end of every foll – (12th: 12th: 12th: 10th: –) row until there are – (71: 73: 75: 77: –) sts.

All sizes

69 (71: 73: 75: 77: 79) sts.

Work even until sleeve measures 14 (14: 14½: 14½: 14½: 15)in (36: 36: 37: 37: 37: 38)cm from cast-on edge, ending with RS facing for next row.

Shape cap

Bind off 4 (5: 5: 6: 6: 7) sts at beg of next 2 rows and 3 sts at beg of foll 2 rows—*55 (55: 57: 57: 59: 59) sts*. Dec 1 st at each end of next 3 rows and foll 2 alt rows, then on every foll 4th row until 35 (35: 37: 37: 39: 39) sts rem. Work even for 1 row, ending with RS facing for next row. Dec 1 st at each end of next and every foll alt rows until 29 sts rem,

then on foll row, ending with RS facing for next row—*27 sts*. Bind off 3 sts at beg of next 4 rows. Bind off rem 15 sts.

To finish

Weave in any loose yarn ends. Steam garment gently. Sew shoulder seams. Sew sleeve heads to armholes. Sew sleeve and side seams.

Neckband

Using 3mm needles and two strands of yarn tog, and with RS facing, rib 5 from right front holder, pick up k 18 (19: 19: 21: 21: 21) sts up right front neck, 31 (33: 33: 35: 35: 35) sts across back neck, and 18 (19: 19: 21: 21: 21) sts down left front neck, then rib 5 from holder —*77 (81: 81: 87: 87: 87) sts*. Work 1 in (2.5cm) in k1, p1 rib as set by front bands. Bind off in rib. Sew press-studs, evenly spaced, to inside of front bands, including neckband.

mademoiselle jacket

materials

Any medium-weight silk-blend yarn, such as Rowan *RYC Natural Silk Aran*

12 (13, 14, 15, 16, 17) × 1¾ oz (50g) balls

Pair each of sizes 6 (4mm) and 7 (4.5mm) knitting needles

Approximately 3¼ yds (3m) of narrow grosgrain ribbon in each of two colors

sizes

to fit bust	32	34	36	38	40	42	in
	81	86	91	97	102	107	cm
actual bust	34	36	38	40.5	42.5	45	in
	86	92	97	103	108	114	cm
length	18½	19	19½	19½	20	20½	in
	47	48	49	50	51	52	cm
sleeve seam	15	15½	15½	15½	16½	16½	in
	38	39.5	39.5	39.5	42	42	cm

gauge

19 sts and 25 rows = 4 in (10cm) over St st using size 7 (4.5mm) needles or whatever size necessary to obtain gauge

See pages 26–27

pattern notes

- Work increases and decreases at armholes, neck, and on pockets three stitches inside the edges to create a fully fashioned detail. Wor the decreases through the back of loops as foll:
  On a k row: K3, k2tog, k to last 5 sts, k2tog tbl, k3.
  On a p row: P3, p2tog tbl, p to last 5 sts, p2tog, p3.
- As row edges of fronts form actual finished edge of garment, it is important that all new balls of yarn are joined in at side seam or armhole edges of rows.

Back

Using size 6 (4mm) needles, cast on 72 (76: 80: 84: 88: 92) sts.

K 4 rows.

Change to size 7 (4.5mm) needles and cont in St st with rib borders for side slits as foll:

Next row (RS): P1, k1, p1, M1, k to last 3 sts, M1, p1, k1, p1.

Next row: K1, p1, k1, p to last 3 sts, k1, p1, k1.

Rep last 2 rows 3 times more—*80 (84: 88: 92: 96: 100) sts.*

This completes side-slit borders.

Cont in St st only throughout, dec 1 st at each end of 7th row and every foll 7th (8th: 8th: 8th: 9th: 9th) row until 74 (78: 82: 86: 90: 94) sts rem.

Work even for 15 (17: 17: 19: 19: 19) rows, ending with RS facing for next row.

Inc 1 st at each end of next row and every foll 7th (8th: 8th: 9th: 9th: 9th) row until there are 80 (84: 88: 92: 96: 100) sts.

Work even until back measures 11¼ (11½: 11½: 11: 11: 11)in (29: 29: 29: 28.5: 28: 28)cm from cast-on edge, ending with RS facing for next row.

Shape armholes

Bind off 4 (4: 4: 5: 5: 5) sts at beg of next 2 rows—*72 (76: 80: 82: 86: 90) sts.*

Dec 1 st at each end of next 3 (3: 3: 3: 4: 4) rows, then on foll 2 alt rows—*62 (66: 70: 72: 74: 78) sts.*

Work even until armhole measures 7¼ (7½: 8: 8½: 9: 9½)in (18: 19: 20: 21.5: 23: 24)cm, ending with RS facing for next row.

Shape shoulders and neck

Bind off 5 (6: 6: 6: 6: 7) sts at beg of next 2 rows—*52 (54: 58: 60: 62: 64) sts.*

Next row (RS): Bind off 5 (6: 7: 6: 7: 7) sts, k until there are 9 (9: 9: 10: 10: 11) sts on right-hand needle, then turn, leaving rem sts on a holder.

Bind off 3 sts at beg of next row.

Bind off rem 6 (6: 6: 7: 7: 8) sts.

With RS of work facing, rejoin yarn to rem sts and bind off center 24 (24: 26: 28: 28: 28) sts, then k to end.

Complete to match first side, reversing all shaping.

Right front

Using size 6 (4mm) needles, cast on 36 (38: 40: 42: 44: 46) sts.

K 4 rows.

Change to size 7 (4.5mm) needles and cont in St st with rib borders as foll:

Next row (RS): P1, k1, p1, k to last 3 sts, M1, p1, k1, p1.

Next row: K1, p1, k1, p to last 3 sts, k1, p1, k1.

Rep last 2 rows 3 times—*40 (42: 44: 46: 48: 50) sts.*

This completes side-slit border.

Cont in St st throughout and keeping 3 rib sts as set along center front only (beg of RS rows and end of WS rows), dec 1 st at side edge only on 7th row and every foll 7th (8th: 8th: 8th: 9th: 9th) row until 37 (39: 41: 43: 45: 47) sts rem.

Work even for 15 (17: 17: 19: 19: 19) rows, ending with RS facing for next row.

Inc 1 st at side edge on next row and every foll 7th (8th: 8th: 9th: 9th: 9th) row until there are 40 (42: 44: 46: 48: 50) sts.

Work even until front measures 11¼ (11½: 11½: 11: 11: 11)in (29: 29: 29: 28.5: 28: 28)cm from cast-on edge, ending with WS facing for next row.

Shape armhole

Bind off 4 (4: 4: 5: 5: 5) sts at beg of row—*36 (38: 40: 41: 43: 45) sts.*

Dec 1 st at armhole edge of next 3 rows, then on foll 2 alt rows—

31: 33: 35: 36: 38: 40) sts.
Work even until armhole measures
4¼ (4¼: 5: 5½: 5¾: 6)in (11: 11:
12.5: 14: 14.5: 15)cm, ending with
RS facing for next row.
Shape neck
Bind off 6 (6: 7: 7: 8: 8) sts at beg
of next row—25 (27: 28: 29: 30:
32) sts.
Dec 1 st at neck edge of next 7
rows, then on foll 2 (2: 2: 3: 3: 3) alt
rows—16 (18: 19: 19: 20: 22) sts.
Work even until armhole matches
back to shoulder shaping, ending at
armhole edge.
Shape shoulder
Bind off 5 (6: 6: 6: 6: 7) sts at beg
of next row and 5 (6: 7: 6: 7: 7) sts
at beg of foll alt row.
Work even for 1 row.
Bind off rem 6 (6: 6: 7: 7: 8) sts.

Left front
Using size 6 (4mm) needles, cast on
36 (38: 40: 42: 44: 46) sts.
K 4 rows.
Change to size 7 (4.5mm) needles
and cont in St st with rib borders
as foll:
Next row (RS): p1, k1, p1, M1,
k to last 3 sts, p1, k1, p1.
Next row: K1, p1, k1, p to last 3

sts, k1, p1, k1.
Rep last 2 rows three times more—
40 (42: 44: 46: 48: 50) sts.
This completes side-slit border.
now completed.
Cont in St st throughout and
keeping 3 rib sts as set along center
front only (end of RS rows and beg
of WS rows), dec 1 st at side edge
only on 7th row and every foll
7th (8th: 8th: 8th: 9th: 9th) row
until 37 (39: 41: 43: 45: 47) sts rem.
Work even for 15 (17: 17: 19: 19:
19) rows, ending with RS facing for
next row.
Inc 1 st at side edge on next row
and every foll 7th (8th: 8th: 9th:
9th: 9th) row until there are 40 (42:
44: 46: 48: 50) sts.
Work even until front measures
11¼ (11½: 11½: 11: 11: 11)in (29:
29: 29: 28.5: 28: 28)cm from cast-
on edge, ending with RS facing for
next row.
Shape armhole
Bind off 4 (4: 4: 5: 5: 5) sts at beg
of row—36 (38: 40: 41: 43: 45) sts.
Dec 1 st at armhole edge of next
3 rows, then on foll 2 alt rows—
31 (33: 35: 36: 38: 40) sts.
Work even until armhole measures
4¼ (4¼: 5: 5½: 5¾: 6)in (11: 11:

12.5: 14: 14.5: 15)cm, ending at
center front edge.
Shape neck
Bind off 6 (6: 7: 7: 8: 8) sts at beg of
next row—25 (27: 28: 29: 30: 32) sts.
Dec 1 st at neck edge of next 7
rows, then on foll 2 (2: 2: 3: 3: 3) alt
rows—16 (18: 19: 19: 20: 22) sts.
Work even until armhole matches
back to shoulder shaping, ending at
armhole edge.
Shape shoulder
Bind off 5 (6: 6: 6: 6: 7) sts at beg
of next row and 5 (6: 7: 6: 7: 7) sts
at end of foll alt row.
Work even for 1 row.
Bind off rem 6 (6: 7: 7: 8) sts.

Sleeves (make 2)
To make cuff slit, use 2 balls of
yarn to cast on as foll:
Using size 6 (4mm) needles, cast on
21 (22: 22: 23: 23: 24) sts with one
ball and 21 (22: 22: 23: 23: 24) sts
with 2nd ball onto same needle.
Working both sides of slit
separately but at same time, k 4
rows.
Change to size 7 (4.5mm) needles.
Next row (RS): K to last 3 sts, p1,
k1, p1 on first piece; then on 2nd
piece, p1, k1, p1, k to end of row.

Next row: Rib sts as set and p
rem sts.

Rep last 2 rows once more.

Next row (inc row) (RS): K to last
3 sts, M1, p1, k1, p1 on first piece;
then on 2nd piece, p1, k1, p1, M1,
k to end.

Cont in rib and St st as set, inc 1 st
on each piece as before on foll 6th
row—*23 (24: 24: 25: 25: 26) sts on
each piece.*

Work even for 1 row as set on both
pieces, ending with RS facing for
next row.

To join pieces, k across all sts using
the first ball of yarn—*46 (48: 48: 50:
50: 52) sts.*

Break off 2nd ball of yarn.

P 1 row.

Cont in St st throughout, inc 1 st at
each end of next row and every foll
12th row until there are 60 (62: 62:
64: 64: 66) sts.

Work even until sleeve measures
15 (15½: 15½: 15½: 16½: 16½)in (38:
39.5: 39.5: 39.5: 42: 42)cm from cast-
on edge, ending with RS facing for
next row.

Shape cap

Bind off 4 (4: 4: 5: 5: 5) sts at beg of
next 2 rows—*52 (54: 54: 54: 54: 56) sts.*

Dec 1 st each end of next 4 rows,

then on foll 2 alt rows, then every
4th row until 34 (34: 32: 32: 30: 30)
sts rem.

P 1 row.

Dec 1 st at each end of next and
every foll alt row until 26 (28: 28: 28:
28: 28) sts rem, then on foll 3 rows—
20 (22: 22: 22: 22: 22) sts.

Bind off 3 sts at beg of next 4 rows—
8 (10: 10: 10: 10: 10) sts.

Bind off rem 8 (10: 10: 10: 10: 10) sts.

Small pockets (make 2)

Using size 7 (4.5mm) needles, cast on
11 (11: 11: 13: 13: 13) sts.

***Row 1 (RS):** P1, k1, p1, k to last
3 sts, p1, k1, p1.

Row 2: K1, p1, k1, p to last 3 sts, k1,
p1, k1.

Row 3: P1, k1, p1, M1, k to last 3
sts, M1, p1, k1, p1.

Row 4: Rep row 2.***

Rep last 2 rows until there are 17 (17:
17: 19: 19: 19) sts.

Keeping 3 rib sts as set at each side
and working rem sts in St st, work
even until pocket measures 3 (3: 3:
3½: 3½: 3½)in (7.5: 7.5: 7.5: 9: 9:
9)cm, ending WS facing for next row.

Change to size 6 (4mm) needles and
k 3 rows.

Bind off knitwise.

Large pockets (make 2)

Using size 7 (4.5mm) needles, cast on
15 (15: 15: 17: 17: 17) sts.

Work as for small pockets from ***
to ***.

Rep last 2 rows until there are 21 (21:
21: 23: 23: 23) sts.

Keeping 3 rib sts as set at each side
and working rem sts in St st, work
even until pocket measures 3½ (3½:
3½: 4: 4: 4)in (9: 9: 9: 10: 10: 10)cm,
ending with WS facing for next row.

Change to size 6 (4mm) needles and
k 3 rows. Bind off knitwise.

To finish

Weave in any loose yarn ends.

Gently press and steam.

Sew shoulder seams.

Sew sleeve heads to armholes.

Sew side seams and sleeve seams,
leaving slits open.

Sew on pockets.

Sew ribbons (with one color slightly
overlapping the other as shown in
photograph) to tops of large pockets
and all around edges, along both
fronts and neckline, and around cuff
edge, taking particular care to trace
around cuff slits.

Sew top of cuff slit sleeve vent
together with a little stitch.

slouch socks

materials

Any medium-weight wool yarn, such as Rowan *RYC Cashsoft Aran*
   or Debbie Bliss *Cashmerino Aran*
   3 (4) × 1 ¾ oz (50g) balls
Pair each of sizes 7 (4.5mm) and 8 (5mm) knitting needles

size

One size, to fit woman's average-size foot (the length of the foot
   can be lengthed or shortened by working more or fewer rows
   where indicated)

gauge

19 sts and 25 rows to 4in/10cm over St st using size 7 (4.5mm) needles
   or whatever size necessary to obtain gauge
18 sts and 24 rows to 4in/10cm over St st using size 8 (5mm) needles or
   whatever size necessary to obtain gauge

pattern note

• Knit the long socks shown in the photograph, or follow the
  alternative instructions for the short socks.

See pages 28–29

slouch socks

Short socks

Right sock

Using size 8 (5mm) needles, cast on 40 sts.

Work 2½ in (6.5cm) in k1, p1 rib. Change to size 7 (4.5mm) needles and cont in rib as set until rib measures 5 in (12.5cm).

Beg with a k row, work in St st until sock measures 7¾ in (19.5cm) from cast-on edge, ending with RS facing for next row.

Shape heel

Next row (RS): K2, k2tog, k12, k2tog tbl, k2, then turn, leaving rem 20 sts on a holder.

Next row: P.

Next row: K2, k2tog, k to last 4 sts, k2tog tbl, k2.

Next row: P.

Rep last 2 rows until 8 sts rem.

Next row (RS): K2, M1, k to last 2 sts, M1, k2.

Next row: P.

Rep last 2 rows until there are 20 sts on needle.

Next row: K 20 sts on needle, then k 20 sts from holder—*40 sts.*

Work even for 5 in (12.5cm), ending with RS facing for next row.

Note: Adjust length of sock here by working more or fewer rows even.

Shape toe

Next row (RS): K2, k2tog, k12, k2tog tbl, k2, then turn, leaving rem 20 sts on a holder.

Next row: P.

Next row: K2, k2tog, k to last 4 sts, k2tog tbl, k2.

Next row: P.

Rep last 2 rows once more—*14 sts.* Dec 1 st at each end of next 3 rows as set—*8 sts.*

P 1 row.

Bind off.

With RS facing, rejoin yarn to rem 20 sts on holder and complete to match first side.

Left sock

Using size 8 (5mm) needles, cast on 40 sts and work 2½ in (6.5cm) in k1, p1 rib.

Change to size 7 (4.5mm) needles and cont in rib as set until rib measures 5 in (12.5cm).

Beg with a k row, work in St st until sock measures 7¾ in (19.5cm) from cast-on edge, ending with WS facing for next row.

Next row: P20, then turn, leaving rem sts on a holder.

Shape heel

Next row: K2, k2tog, k12, k2tog tbl, k2.

Next row: P.

Next row: K2, k2tog, k to last 4 sts, k2tog tbl, k2.

Next row: P.

Rep last 2 rows until 8 sts rem.

Next row (RS): K2, M1, k to last 2 sts, M1, k2.

Next row: P.

Next row: K2, M1, k to last 2 sts, M1, k2.

Rep last 2 rows until there are 20 sts on needle.

Next row: P 20 sts on needle, then p 20 sts from holder—*40 sts.*

Work even for 5 in (12.5cm), ending with RS facing for next row.

Note: Adjust length of sock here by working more or fewer rows even.

Shape toe

Next row (RS): K2, k2tog, k12, k2tog tbl, k2, then turn, leaving rem 20 sts on a holder.

Next row: P.

Next row: K2, k2tog, k to last 4 sts, k2tog tbl, k2.

Next row: P.

Rep last 2 rows once more—*14 sts.* Dec 1 st at each end of next 3 rows as set—*8 sts.*

P 1 row. Bind off.

With RS facing, rejoin yarn to rem 20 sts on holder and complete to match first side.

Long socks

Right sock

Using size 8 (5mm) needles, cast on 46 sts.

Work 5 in (12.5cm) in k1, p1 rib.
Change to size 7 (4.5mm) needles and beg with a k row, work in St st, dec 1 st each end of 19th row and every foll 20th row until 40 sts rem.

Work even until sock measures 15 in (38cm) from cast-on edge, ending with RS facing for next row.

Shape heel

Next row: K2, k2tog, k12, k2tog tbl, k2, then turn, leaving rem 20 sts on a holder.

Next row: P.

Next row: K2, k2tog, k to last 4 sts, k2tog tbl, k2.

Next row: P.

Rep last 2 rows until 8 sts rem.

Next row (RS): K2, M1, k to last 2 sts, M1, k2.

Next row: P.

Rep last 2 rows until there are 20 sts on needle.

Next row (RS): K 20 sts on needle, then k 20 sts from holder—*40 sts.*

Work even for 5 in (12.5cm), ending with RS facing for next row.

Note: Adjust length of sock here by working more or fewer rows even.

Shape toe

Next row: K2, k2tog, k12, k2tog tbl, k2, then turn, leaving rem 20 sts on a holder.

Next row: P.

Next row: K2, k2tog, k to last 4 sts, k2tog tbl, k2.

Next row: P.

Rep last 2 rows once more—*14 sts.*

Dec 1 st at each end of next 3 rows as set—*8 sts.*

P 1 row.

Bind off.

With RS facing, rejoin yarn to rem 20 sts on holder and complete to match first side.

Left sock

Using size 8 (5mm) needles, cast on 46 sts.

Work 5 in (12.5cm) in k1, p1 rib.
Change to size 7 (4.5mm) needles and beg with a k row, work in St st, dec 1 st at each end of 19th row and every foll 20th row until 40 sts rem.

Work even until sock measures 15 in (38cm) from cast-on edge, ending with WS facing for next row.

Next row (WS): P20, then turn, leaving rem sts on a holder.

Shape heel

Next row: K2, k2tog, k12, k2tog tbl, k 2.

Next row: P.

Next row: K2, k2tog, k to last 4 sts, k2tog tbl, k2.

Next row: P.

Rep last 2 rows until 8 sts rem.

Next row (RS): K2, M1, k to last 2 sts, M1, k2.

Next row: P.

Next row: K2, M1, k to last 2 sts, M1, k2.

Rep last 2 rows until there are 20 sts on needle.

Next row: P 20 sts on needle, then p 20 sts from holder—*40 sts.*

Work even for 5 in (12.5cm), ending with RS facing for next row.

Note: Adjust length of sock here by working more or fewer rows even.

Shape toe

Next row: K2, k2tog, k12, k2tog tbl, k2, then turn, leaving rem 20 sts on a holder.

Next row: P.

Next row: K2, k2tog, k to last 4 sts, k2tog tbl, k 2.

Next row: P.

Rep last 2 rows once more—*14 sts.*

Dec 1 st at each end of next 3 rows as set—*8 sts.*

P 1 row.

Bind off.

With RS facing, rejoin yarn to rem 20 sts on holder and complete to match first side.

To finish

Weave in any loose yarn ends.
Lay work out flat and gently steam to enhance yarn.
Sew two heel seams first.
Sew side seam, starting at toe with an invisible seam and reversing seam on turnover part of rib.

cotton camisole

materials

Any fine-weight mercerized cotton yarn, such as Yeoman's
  Cotton Cannele 4ply
  2 × 8¾ oz (250g) cones or 1395 (1488, 1580, 1673, 1766, 1860) yds
  (1275, 1360, 1445, 1530, 1615, 1700)m
Pair each of sizes 2 (3mm) and 3 (3.25mm) knitting needles
Cable needle

sizes

to fit bust	32	34	36	38	40	42	in
	81	86	91	97	102	107	cm
actual bust	32	34	36	38	40	42	in
	81	86	91	97	102	107	cm
length	18	19	20	21	22	23	in
	46	48	51	53	5	58.5	cm

gauge

29 sts and 36 rows = 4 in (10cm) over St st using size 3 (3.25mm) needles
  or whatever size necessary to obtain gauge

See pages 30–31

stitches

decreasing with an eyelet
K3, k2tog, yo, k2tog, k to last 7 sts, k2tog tbl, yo, k2tog tbl, k3.

increasing with an eyelet
K3, yo, k to last 3 sts, yo, k3.

C4F (cable 4 front)
Slip next 2 sts onto cn and leave at front of work, k2, then k2 from cn.

Back
Using size 2 (3mm) needles, cast on 108 (114: 120: 126: 132: 138) sts. Work ¾ in (2cm) in k1, p1 rib. Change to size 3 (3.25mm) needles and St st, dec 1 st with an eyelet at each end of 5th row and every foll 6th row until 100 (106: 112: 118: 124: 130) sts rem.
Work even for 19 (19: 21: 21: 23: 23) rows, ending with RS facing for next row.
Cont in St st throughout, inc 1 st with an eyelet at each end of next row and every foll 6th (6th: 6th: 8th: 8th: 8th) row until there are 116 (122: 128: 134: 140: 146) sts.
Work even until back measures 10 (10½: 11: 11½: 12: 12½)in (25.5: 26.5: 28.5: 30: 30.5: 32)cm from cast-on edge, ending with RS facing for next row.

Divide for neck
**Working each side separately, divide for neck as foll:
Next row (RS): K55 (58: 61: 64: 67: 70), p1, k1, p1, then turn, leaving rem 58 (61: 64: 67: 70: 73) sts on a holder.
Next row: K1, p1, k1, p to end.
Next row (dec row): K to last 5 sts, k2tog tbl, p1, k1, p1.
***Keeping neck rib border as set, cont to dec 1 st as set at neck edge on every alt row **and at the same time** when back measures 11 (11½: 12: 12½: 13: 13½)in (28: 29: 31: 32.5: 33: 34.5)cm from cast-on edge, ending with RS facing, shape armhole as foll:

Shape armhole
Bind off 5 sts at beg of next row.
Work even for 1 row.
Dec 1 st at armhole edge on next 9 rows, then on foll 7 alt rows, using an eyelet decrease on first of these decreases and every foll 4th row.
Cont dec as set at neck edge only on alt rows until 10 (10: 10: 10: 12: 12) sts rem.
Work even ribbing across all sts as set until armhole measures 7 (7½: 8: 8½: 9: 9½)in (18: 19: 20: 21.5: 23: 24)cm.

Bind off in rib.

With RS facing. rejoin yarn to sts on holder and cont as foll:

Next row: P1, k1, p1, k to end of row.

Next row: P to last 3 sts, k1, p1, k1.

Next row (dec row): P1, k1, p1, k2tog, k to end.

Complete to match first side from ***, reversing all shaping.

Front

Work as for back **and at the same time** 24 rows before start of neck shaping, place a marker at center of sts and cont with side increases as set, work as foll:

Row 1: K to 3 sts before marker, p1, C4F, p1, k to end.

Row 2: P to 3 sts before marker, k1, p4, k1, p to end.

Row 3: K to 3 sts before marker, p1, k4, p1, k to end.

Row 4: Rep row 2.

Rep rows 1–4 once more, then rows 1 and 2 again.

Row 11: K.

Row 12: P.

Row 13: K to marker, yo, k to end.

Row 14: P, move marker to center st.

Row 15: K.

Row 16: P.

Row 17: K to marker, p1, k to end.

Row 18: P to 1 st before marker, k1, p1, k1, p to end.

Row 19: K to 2 sts before marker, p1, k1, p1, k1, p1, k to end.

Row 20: P to 1 st before marker, k1, p1, k1, p to end.

Row 21: K to marker, p1, k to end.

Row 22: P.

Row 23: K.

Row 24: P58 (61: 64: 67: 70: 73), p2tog, p to end of row—*116 (122: 128: 134: 140: 146) sts*.

Complete as for back from **.

To finish

Weave in any loose yarn ends.

Gently steam and press pieces under a damp cloth.

Sew shoulder seams with a flat seam.

Sew side seams.

silk shrug

materials

Any lightweight silk yarn, such as Jaeger *Silk DK*
   6 (6, 6, 7, 7, 8) × 1¾ oz (50g) balls
Pair each of sizes 3 (3.25mm) and 5 (3.75mm) knitting needles
Size 3 (3.25mm) circular knitting needle

sizes

to fit bust	32	34	36	38	40	42	in
	81	86	91	97	102	107	cm
actual bust	34	35	36½	38	39½	40½	in
	85	88	92	95	98	102	cm
length	13	14	14½	15	15½	16	in
	33	35.5	37	38	39	41	cm

gauge

24 sts and 34 rows = 4 in (10cm) over St st using size 5 (3.75mm) needles
   or whatever size necessary to obtain gauge

pattern note

• To create a fully fashioned detail, work increases and decreases
   three stitches inside the edges. Work the decreases through the
   back of loops as foll:
   On a k row: K3, k2tog, k to last 5 sts, k2tog tbl, k3.
   On a p row: P3, p2tog tbl, p to last 5 sts, p2tog, p3.

See pages 32–33

silk shrug

Back

Using size 3 (3.25mm) needles, cast on 90 (94: 98: 102: 106: 110) sts. Work 1½ in (3.5cm) in k1, p1 rib. Change to size 5 (3.75mm) needles and beg with a k row, work in St st, inc 1 st at each end of 9th row and every foll 6th row until there are 102 (106: 110: 114: 118: 122) sts. Cont in St st throughout, work even for 9 (13: 13: 15: 17: 17) rows.

Shape armhole

Bind off 4 (4: 5: 5: 6: 6) sts at beg of next 2 rows.

Dec 1 st at each end of next 9 rows—*76 (80: 82: 86: 88: 92) sts.* Work even for 45 (49: 53: 57: 57: 61) rows.

Shape shoulders

Bind off 12 (13: 13: 13: 13: 14) sts at beg of next 2 rows and 13 (13: 13: 14: 14: 14) sts at beg of foll 2 rows.

Bind off rem 26 (28: 30: 32: 34: 36) sts.

Right front

Using size 5 (3.75mm) needles, cast on 7 (9: 11: 13: 15: 17) sts.

Row 1 (RS): K.

Row 2: P to last 3 sts, p into front and back of next st, p2.

Row 3: K1, k into front and back of next st, k to end.

Rows 4–7: Rep rows 2 and 3 twice.

Row 8: Rep row 2.

Row 9: K1, k into front and back of next st, k to last 3 sts, k into front and back of next st, k2.

Row 10: Rep row 2.

Row 11: Rep row 3.

Row 12: Rep row 2.

Row 13: Rep row 3.

Row 14: Rep row 2.

Rep rows 9–14 twice.

Rep rows 9–11 once.

Cont in St st throughout, work 20

(24: 24: 26: 28: 28) rows, inc 1 st at end of 4th and 10th rows as set, ending with WS facing for next row—*41 (43: 45: 47: 49: 51) sts.*

Shape armhole

**Bind off 5 (6: 7: 8: 8: 8) sts at beg of next row.

Dec 1 st at armhole edge on next 11 (11: 12: 12: 15: 15) rows—*25 (26: 26: 27: 27: 28) sts.* Work even until armhole matches back to shoulder shaping, ending with ws facing for next row.

Shape shoulder

Bind off 12 (13: 13: 13: 14: 14) sts at beg of next row.

Work 1 row.

Bind off rem 13 (13: 13: 14: 14: 14) sts.**

Left front

Using size 5 (3.75mm) needles, cast on 7 (9: 11: 13: 15: 17) sts.

Row 1 (RS): K.

Row 2: P1, p into front and back of next st, p to end.

Row 3: K to last 3 sts, k into front and back of next st, k2.

Rows 4–7: Rep rows 2 and 3 twice.

Row 8: Rep row 2.

Row 9: K1, k into front and back of next st, k to last 3 sts, k into front and back of next st, k2.

Row 10: Rep row 2.

Row 11: Rep row 3.

Row 12: Rep row 2.

Row 13: Rep row 3.

Row 14: Rep row 2.

Rep rows 9–14 twice.

Rep rows 9–11 once.

Cont in St st throughout, work 19 (23: 23: 25: 27: 27) rows, inc 1 st at beg of 4th and 10th rows as set, ending with RS facing for next row—*41 (43: 45: 47: 49: 51) sts.*

Complete as for right front from ** to **.

Sleeves

Using size 3 (3.25mm) needles, cast on 72 (76: 80: 84: 88: 92) sts.

Work 1½ in (3.5cm) in k1, p1 rib.

Change to size 5 (3.75mm) needles and beg with a k row, work in St st, shaping sleeve top as foll:

Dec 1 st each end of next 5 rows— *62 (66: 70: 74: 78: 82) sts.*

Dec 1 st at each end of every foll alt row until 28 (30: 32: 34: 36: 38) sts rem.

Work 1 row.

Dec 1 st at each end of next 4 rows.

Bind off 3 sts at beg of next 4 rows.

Bind off rem 8 (10: 12: 14: 16: 18) sts.

To finish

Weave in any loose yarn ends.

Lay work out flat and gently steam.

Sew both shoulder seams.

Front bands

Using size 3 (3.25mm) circular needle and with RS of right front facing, rejoin yarn at side edge and pick up and k 112 (118: 124: 130: 136: 142) sts up right front, 26 (28: 30: 32: 34: 36) sts across back neck, and 112 (118: 124: 130: 136: 142) sts down left front—*250 (264: 278: 292: 306: 320) sts.*

Working in rows rather than rounds, work 1½ in (3.5cm) in k1, p1 rib.

Bind off in rib.

To finish

Sew sleeve heads into armholes with an invisible seam.

Join side seams with an invisible seam.

gloves

materials

Any double-knitting-weight cotton-blend yarn, such as Rowan
  RYC Cashcotton DK
  Two 1½ oz (50g) balls
Pair each of sizes 2 (3mm) and 3 (3.25mm) knitting needles

size

One size, to fit worman' average-size hand

gauge

25 sts and 34 rows = 4 in (10cm) over St st using size 3 (3.25mm) needles
  or whatever size necessary to obtain gauge

pattern note

• As an alternative, instructions are given for fingerless gloves as well.

See pages 34–35

Gloves

Right glove
Using size 2 (3mm) needles, cast on
44 sts.
Work 3¼ in (8cm) in k1, p1 rib.
Change to size 3 (3.25mm) needles
and beg with a k row, work 8 rows
in St st.
Shape thumb
Row 1 (RS): K21, p1, k into front
and back of next st, k1, k into
front and back of next st, p1, k18—
46 sts.
Row 2: P18, k1, p5, k1, p21.
Row 3: K21, p1, k5, p1, k18.
Row 4: Rep row 2.
Row 5: K21, p1, k into front and
back of next st, k3, k into front and
back of next st, p1, k18—*48 sts.*
Cont to inc 1 st at each side of
thumb gusset on every 4th row until
there are 56 sts, keeping p st at
either side to define shaping.
Work even for 1 row.
Next row: K37, turn, cast on 2 sts.
Next row: P16, turn, cast on 2 sts
—*18 sts.*
**Work 16 rows on these 18 sts.
Next row: K1, [k2, k2tog] 4 times,
k1.
Next row: P.

Next row: [K2tog] 5 times, k4—
9 sts.
Break off yarn leaving a long end,
thread through rem sts, gather
tightly, secure firmly, then sew
thumb seam.
With right-hand needle, rejoin yarn
and pick up and k 4 sts at base of
thumb, then k to end of row—
46 sts.
Work 11 rows.
Shape first finger
Next row: K29, turn, cast on 1 st.
Next row: P13, turn, cast on 1 st
—*14 sts.*
Work 22 rows on these 14 sts.
Next row: K1, [k2, k2tog] 3 times,
k1.
Next row: P.
Next row: K2, [k2tog] 4 times, k1
—*7 sts.*
Break off yarn leaving a long end,
thread through rem sts, gather
tightly, secure firmly, then sew
finger seam.
Shape second finger
With right-hand needle, rejoin yarn
and pick up and k 2 sts at base of
first finger, then k6, turn, cast on
1 st.
Next row: P15, turn, cast on 1 st
—*16 sts.*

Work 26 rows.
Next row: K2, [k2tog, k2] 3 times,
k2.
Next row: P.
Next row: K1, [k2tog] 6 times
—*7 sts.*
Complete as for first finger.
Shape third finger
With right-hand needle, rejoin yarn
and pick up and k 2 sts at base of
second finger, then k6, turn, cast on
1 st.
Next row: P15, turn, cast on 1 st
—*16 sts.*
Work 22 rows.
Complete as for second finger.
Shape fourth finger
With right-hand needle, rejoin
yarn and pick up and k 2 sts at base
of third finger, then k5—*12 sts.*
Work 19 rows.
Next row: K2, [k2, k2tog] twice,
k2.
Next row: P.
Next row: [K2tog] 5 times—*5 sts.*
Complete as for second finger and
sew down side seam to wrist.**

Left glove
Work to match right glove,
reversing position of thumb gusset
by shaping as foll:

Row 1 (RS): K18, p1, k into front and back of next st, k1, k into front and back of next st, p1, k21—*46 sts.*
Row 2: P21, k1, p5, k1, p18.
Row 3: K18, p1, k5, p1, k21.
Row 4: Rep row 2.
Row 5: K18, p1, k into front and back of next st, k3, k into front and back of next st, p1, k21—*48 sts.*
Cont to inc 1 st at each side of thumb gusset on every 4th row until there are 56 sts, keeping p st at either side to define shaping.
Work even for 1 row.
Next row: K34, turn, cast on 2 sts.
Next row: P16, turn, cast on 2 sts —*18 sts.*
Complete as for right glove, working from ** to **.

To finish
Steam gloves to enhance the yarn. Sew side seam and finger seams with mattress st for invisible finish.

Fingerless gloves

Right glove
Using size 2 (3mm) needles, cast on 44 sts.
Work 2¼ in (5.5cm) in k1, p1 rib.
Change to size 3 (3.25mm) needles

and cont in rib as set until work measures 5½ in (14cm) from cast-on edge, ending with RS facing for next row.

Shape thumb gussett
Row 1 (RS): K21, p1, k into front and back of next st, k1, k into front and back of next st, p1, k18—*46 sts.*
Row 2: P18, k1, p5, k1, p21.
Row 3: K21, p1, k5, p1, k18.
Row 4: Rep row 2.
Row 5: K21, p1, k into front and back of next st, k3, k into front and back of next st, p1, k18—*48 sts.*
Cont to inc 1 st each side of thumb gusset on every 4th row until there are 56 sts, keeping p st at either side to define shaping.
Work even for 1 row.
Next row: K37, turn, cast on 2 sts.
Next row: P16, turn, cast on 2 sts —*18 sts.*
**Work 4 rows St st, then 4 rows of k1, p1 rib on these 18 sts.
Bind off in rib.
Break off yarn leaving a long end and sew thumb seam.
With right-hand needle, rejoin yarn and pick up and k 4 sts at base of thumb, then k to end of row—*46 sts.*
Work 9 rows in St st.
Work 4 rows in k1, p1 rib.

Bind off in rib.
Break off yarn leaving a long end to sew side seam.**

Left glove
Work to match right glove, reversing position of thumb gusset as foll:

Row 1 (RS): K18, p1, k into front and back of next st, k1, k into front and back of next st, p1, k21—*46 sts.*
Row 2: P21, k1, p5, k1, p18.
Row 3: K18, p1, k5, p1, k21.
Row 4: Rep row 2.
Row 5: K18, p1, k into front and back of next st, k3, k into front and back of next st, p1, k21—*48 sts.*
Cont to inc 1 st at each side of thumb gusset on every 4th row until there are 56 sts, keeping p st at either side to define shaping.
Work even for 1 row.
Next row: K34, turn, cast on 2 sts.
Next row: P16, turn, cast on 2 sts—*18 sts.*
Complete as for right glove, working from ** to **.

To finish
Steam gloves to enhance the yarn. Sew the side seam with mattress st for invisible finish.

deep v sweater

materials

Any lightweight cotton-blend yarn, such as Debbie Bliss *Cathay*
   10 (11, 11, 12, 12, 13) × 1¾ oz (50g) balls
Pair each of sizes 3 (3mm) and 5 (3.75mm) knitting needles

sizes

to fit bust	32	34	36	38	40	42	in
	81	86	91	97	102	107	cm
actual bust	34	36	38	40½	42½	45	in
	86	92	97	103	108	114	cm
length	22	23	23	24	24	25	in
	56	58	58	61	61	63.5	cm
sleeve seam	17½	18	18	18½	18½	19	in
	44.5	46	46	47	47	48	cm

gauge

22 sts and 30 rows = 4 in (10cm) over St st using size 5 (3.75mm) needles
   or whatever size necessary to obtain gauge

pattern notes

• To create a fully fashioned detail, work increases and decreases
   three stitches inside the edges. Work decreases through the back
   of loops as foll:
   On a k row: K3, k2tog, k to last 5 sts, k2tog tbl, k3.
   On a p row: P3, p2tog tbl, p to last 5 sts, p2tog, p3.
• When picking up sts around the neck, pick up and knit one stitch
   for every stitch and 3 stitches for every 4 rows.

See pages 36–37

deep v sweater

Back

Using size 3 (3mm) needles, cast on 96 (102: 108: 114: 120: 126) sts. Work 3¾ in (7cm) in k1, p1 rib. Change to size 5 (3.75mm) needles and beg with a k row, work in St st, dec 1 st at each end of 9th (11th: 11th: 13th: 13th: 15th) row and every foll 12th row until 90 (96: 102: 108: 114: 120) sts rem.

Cont in St st throughout, work even for 19 (21: 21: 23: 23: 25) rows, ending with RS facing for next row. Inc 1 st at each end of next row and every foll 12th row until there are 96 (102: 108: 114: 120: 126) sts. Work even until back measures 14¾ (15½: 15: 15¾: 15½: 16)in (38: 39: 38: 40: 39: 40.5)cm from cast-on edge, ending with RS facing for next row.

Shape armhole

Bind off 5 sts at beg of next 2 rows —86 (92: 98: 104: 110: 116) sts.

Dec 1 st at each end of next 5 rows —76 (82: 88: 94: 100: 106) sts. Dec 1 st at each end of next 3 alt rows—70 (76: 82: 88: 94: 100) sts. Work even until armhole measures 7¼ (7½: 8: 8¼: 8½: 9)in (18: 19: 20: 21: 22: 23)cm, ending with RS facing for next row.

Shape shoulders and neck

Next row (RS): Bind off 8 (9: 10: 11: 12: 13) sts, k until there are 13 (14: 15: 17: 18: 19) sts on right-hand needle, then turn, leaving rem sts on a holder.

Bind off 4 (4: 4: 5: 5: 5) sts at beg of next row.

Bind off rem 9 (10: 11: 12: 13: 14) sts.

With RS of work facing, rejoin yarn and bind off 28 (30: 32: 32: 34: 36) sts, then k to end of row. Complete to match first side, reversing all shaping.

Front

Work as for back, but when work measures 8¾ (9¼: 9¼: 9¾: 9¾: 10)in (22.5: 23.5: 23.5: 24.5: 24.5: 25)cm from cast-on edge, ending with RS facing for next row, divide for neck as foll:

Count number of sts on needle to find center of front and mark center.

Next row: K to center, then turn, leaving rem sts on a holder.

Work side and armhole shaping as for back **and at the same time** working each side of neck separately, shape neck as foll:

P 1 row.

Next row: K to last 5 sts, k2tog tbl, k3.

Dec 1 st at neck edge on every foll 4th row 13 times more, then on every foll 6th row 5 times—17 (19: 21: 23: 25: 27) sts.

Work even until front matches back to shoulder shaping, ending

with RS facing for next row.
Shape shoulders
Bind off 8 (9: 10: 11: 12: 13) sts,
work to end of row.
P 1 row.
Bind off rem 9 (10: 11: 12: 13: 14) sts.
With RS facing, rejoin yarn to rem
sts and k to end.
P 1 row.
Next row: K3, k2tog, k to end.
Complete to match first side,
reversing all shaping.

Sleeves (make 2)
Using size 3 (3mm) needles, cast on
60 (60: 62: 62: 64: 64) sts.
Work 2¾ in (7cm) in k1, p1 rib.
Change to size 5 (3.75mm) needles
and beg with a k row, work in St st,
inc 1 st at each end of 11th row
and every foll 12th row until 76 (76:
78: 78: 80: 80) sts.
Work even until sleeve measures
17½ (18: 18: 18½: 18½: 19)in (44.5:

46: 46: 47: 47: 48)cm from cast-on
edge, ending with RS facing for
next row.
Shape cap
Bind off 5 sts at beg of next 2 rows
—*66 (66: 68: 68: 70: 70) sts.*
Dec 1 st at each end of next 5 rows,
then on every foll alt row until 24 sts
rem.
Dec 1 st at each end of next 5 rows.
Bind off rem 14 sts.

To finish
Weave in any loose yarn ends.
Gently steam to enhance the yarn.
Sew right shoulder seam.
Neckband
Using size 3 (3mm) needles and
with RS facing, pick up and k 75
(77: 77: 81: 81: 85) sts down left
side of neck, place a marker on
needle, pick up and k 75 (77: 77:
81: 81: 85) sts up right side of neck,
and 36 (38: 38: 42: 44: 46) sts across

back neck—*186 (192: 192: 204:
206: 216) sts.*
Work in k1, p1 rib as foll:
Row 1 (WS): Beg with k1, work in
k1, p1 rib over first 111 (115: 115:
123: 125: 131) sts, slip marker to
right-hand needle, beg with k1,
work in k1, p1 rib to end.
Row 2: Rib as set to 2 sts before
marker, k2tog tbl, slip marker to
right-hand needle, k2tog, rib to end.
Row 3: Rib as set to 2 sts before
marker, p2tog, slip marker to right-
hand needle, p2tog tbl, rib to end.
Rep last 2 rows until neckband
measures 1 in (2.5cm).
Bind off in rib.
Sew left shoulder seam.
Sew sleeve heads to armholes
with an invisible seam.
Sew side and sleeve seams with an
invisible seam.

classic turtleneck

materials

Any double-knitting-weight wool yarn, such as Rowan
   RYC Cashsoft DK
   9 (9, 10, 10, 11, 11) × 1¾oz (50g) balls
Pair each of sizes 5 (3.75mm) and 6 (4mm) knitting needles
Size 5 (3.75mm) circular knitting needle, for collar

sizes

to fit bust	32	34	36	38	40	42	in
	81	86	91	97	102	107	cm
actual bust	34	36	38	40½	42½	45	in
	86	92	97	103	108	114	cm
length	22	23	23	24	24	25	in
	56	58	58	61	61	63.5	cm
sleeve seam	17½	18	18	18½	18½	19	in
	44.5	46	46	47	47	48	cm

gauge

22 sts and 30 rows = 4 in (10cm) over St st using size 6 (4mm) needles
   or whatever size necessary to obtain gauge

pattern note

• To create a fully fashioned detail, work increases and decreases
   three stitches inside the edges. Work the decreases through the
   back of loops as foll:
   On a k row: K3, k2tog, k to last 5 sts, k2tog tbl, k3.
   On a p row: P3, p2tog tbl, p to last 5 sts, p2tog, p3.

See pages 38–39

classic turtleneck

Back

With size 5 (3.75mm) needles, cast on 64 (70: 76: 82: 88: 94) sts.

Work 2¼ in (6cm) in St st, ending with RS facing for next row.

Next row (RS): P (to make fold line for hem).

Change to size 6 (4mm) needles and beg with p row, work 2¼ in (6cm) in St st, ending with RS facing for next row.

Next row (RS): To make hem, k tog 1 st from needle and 1 loop from cast-on edge all across row.

Next row: P.**

Next row: K0 (3: 6: 9: 12: 15), *k into front and back of next st, k1, rep from * to last 0 (3: 6: 9: 12: 15), k 0 (3: 6: 9: 12: 15)—*96 (102: 108: 114: 120: 126) sts.*

Cont in St st throughout, work until back measures 14¾ (15½: 15: 15¾: 15½: 16)in (37: 38: 38: 39.5: 39.5: 41)cm from hem fold line row, ending with RS facing for next row.

Shape armholes

Bind off 5 sts at beg of next 2 rows —*86 (92: 98: 104: 110: 116) sts.*

Dec 1 st at each end of next 5 rows —*76 (82: 88: 94: 100: 106) sts.*

Dec 1 st at each end of next 3 alt rows —*70 (76: 82: 88: 94: 100) sts.*

Work even until armhole measures 7¼ (7½: 8: 8¼: 8½: 9)in (18: 19: 20: 21: 22: 23)cm, ending with RS facing for next row.

Shape shoulders and neck

Next row (RS): Bind off 8 (9: 10: 11: 12: 13) sts, k until there are 13 (14: 16: 17: 18: 19) sts on right-hand needle, then turn, leaving rem sts on a holder.

Bind off 4 (4: 5: 5: 5: 5) sts at beg of next row.

Bind off rem 9 (10: 11: 12: 13: 14) sts.

With RS facing, rejoin yarn and slip center 28 (30: 30: 32: 34: 36) sts onto a holder, then rejoin yarn to rem sts and complete to match first side, reversing all shaping.

Front

Work as for back until 12 (12: 14: 14: 14: 16) rows fewer have been worked to start of shoulder shaping, ending with RS facing for next row.

Shape neck

Next row: K25 (27: 30: 32: 34: 37), then turn, leaving rem sts on a holder.

Bind off 4 (4: 4: 5: 5: 5) sts at beg of next row—*21 (23: 26: 27: 29: 32) sts.*

Dec 1 st at neck edge on next 3 rows, then on foll alt rows until 17 (19: 21: 23: 25: 27) sts rem.

Work even for 5 rows, ending with RS facing for next row.

Shape shoulder

Bind off 8 (9: 10: 11: 12: 13) sts at beg of next row.

Work 1 row.

Bind off rem 9 (10: 11: 12: 13: 14) sts. With RS facing, slip center 20 (22: 22: 24: 26: 26) sts onto a holder and rejoin yarn to rem sts, then k to end. Complete to match first side, reversing all shaping and working 1 extra row before start of shoulder shaping.

Sleeves (make 2)

Using size 5 (3.75mm) needles, cast on 35 (38: 41: 44: 47: 50) sts.

Work hem as for back to **.

Next row (RS): K into front and back of every st across row—*70 (76: 82: 88: 94: 100) sts.*

Cont in St st throughout, work until sleeve measures 17½ (18: 18: 18½: 18½: 19)in (44.5: 46: 46: 47: 47: 48)cm from hem fold line row, ending with RS facing for next row.

Shape cap

Bind off 5 sts at beg of next 2 rows —*60 (66: 72: 78: 84: 90) sts.*

Dec 1 st at each end of next 5 rows —*50 (56: 62: 68: 74: 80) sts.*

Dec 1 st at each end of every foll alt row until 20 (24: 26: 32: 36: 40) sts rem then at each end of next 3 (5: 5: 7: 7: 9) rows.

Bind off rem 14 (14: 16: 18: 22: 22) sts.

To finish

Weave in any loose yarn ends.

Sew shoulder seams.

Collar

Using size 5 (3.75mm) needles and with RS facing, pick up and k 16 (16: 19: 19: 19: 20) sts down left front neck, 20 (22: 22: 24: 26: 26) sts from holder, 16 (16: 19: 19: 19: 20) sts up right front neck, 4 (4: 5: 5: 5: 5) sts down right back neck, 28 (30: 30: 32: 34: 36) sts from holder, and 4 (4: 5: 5: 5: 5) sts up left back neck —*88 (92: 100: 104: 108: 112) sts.*

Work in k2, p2 rib for 3½ in (9cm).

Change to size 6 (4mm) needles and work further 3½ in (9cm) more as set.

Bind off in rib.

Weave in any loose yarn ends.

Lay work out flat and steam gently to enhance yarn.

Sew sleeve seams and cuffs with an invisible seam.

Sew side and hem seams with an invisible seam.

Set in sleeves and sew in place.

Sew turtleneck collar seam, reversing seam half way so it will not show when turned over.

yarns

Although I have recommended a specific yarn for many of the projects in the book, you can substitute others. A description of each of the yarns used is given below.

If you decide to use an alternative yarn, purchase a substitute yarn that is as close as possible to the original in thickness, weight, and texture so that it will work with the pattern instructions. Buy only one ball to start with, so you can test the effect. Calculate the number of balls you will need by yards/meters rather than by weight. The recommended knitting-needle size and knitting gauge on the yarn labels provide extra direction to the yarn thickness.

To obtain Debbie Bliss, Rowan (and Jaeger), or Yeoman yarns, go to the websites below to find a mail-order supplier or store in your area:

www.uniquekolours.com for Colinette
www.knitrowan.com for Rowan
www.knittingfever.com for Debbie Bliss
www.yarnups.com for Yeoman Yarns

Debbie Bliss *Cashmerino Aran*
A medium-weight wool-blend yarn
Recommended needle size: size 8 (5mm)
Gauge: 18 sts × 24 rows per 4 in (10cm) over St st
Ball size: 99 yds (90m) per 1¾oz (50g) ball
Yarn specification: 55% merino wool, 33% microfiber, 12% cashmere

Debbie Bliss *Cashmerino Superchunky*
A super-bulky-weight wool-blend yarn
Recommended needle size: size 11 (7.5mm)
Gauge: 12 sts × 17 rows per 4 in (10cm) over St st
Ball size: 82 yds (75m) per 1¾oz (50g) ball
Yarn specification: 55% merino wool, 33% microfiber, 12% cashmere

Debbie Bliss *Cathay*
A lightweight cotton-blend yarn
Recommended needle size: size 5 (3.75mm)
Gauge: 22 sts × 30 rows per 4 in (10cm) over St st
Ball size: 110 yds (100m) per 1¾oz (50g) ball
Yarn specification: 50% cotton, 35% microfiber, 15% silk

Jaeger *Silk DK*
A double-knitting-weight silk yarn
Recommended needle size: size 6 (4mm)
Gauge: 22 sts × 30 rows per 4 in (10cm) over St st
Ball size: 137 yds (125m) per 1¾oz (50g) ball
Yarn specification: 100% silk

Rowan *Big Wool*
A super-bulky-weight wool yarn
Recommended needle size: size 17 (15mm)
Gauge: 7.5 sts × 10 rows per 4 in (10cm) over St st
Ball size: 88 yds (80m) per 3½ oz (100g) ball
Yarn specification: 100% merino wool

Rowan *Kidsilk Haze*
A fine-weight mohair-blend yarn
Recommended needle size: sizes 3–8 (3.25–5mm)
Gauge: 18–25 sts × 23–24 rows per 4 in (10cm) over St st
Ball size: 230 yds (210m) per ¾ oz (25g) ball
Yarn specification: 70% super kid mohair, 30% silk

Rowan *Little Big Wool*
A super-bulky-weight wool yarn
Recommended needle size: size 17 (15mm)
Gauge: 7.5 sts × 10 rows per 4 in (10cm) over St st
Ball size: 88 yds (80m) per 3½ oz (100g) ball
Yarn specification: 100% merino wool

Rowan *RYC Cashcotton DK*
A double-knitting weight cotton-blend yarn
Recommended needle size: size 6 (4mm)
Gauge: 22 sts × 30 rows per 4 in (10cm) over St st
Ball size: 142 yds (130m) per 1¾oz (50g) ball
Yarn specification: 35% cotton, 25% polyamide, 18% angora, 13% viscose, 9% cashmere

Rowan *RYC Cashsoft Aran*
An medium-weight wool-blend yarn
Recommended needle size: size 7 (4.5mm)
Gauge: 19 sts × 25 rows per 4 in (10cm) over St st
Ball size: 95 yds (87m) per 1¾oz (50g) ball
Yarn specification: 57% fine merino wool, 33% microfiber, 10% cashmere

Rowan *RYC Cashsoft DK*

An double-knitting-weight wool-blend yarn

Recommended needle size: size 6 (4mm)
Gauge: 22 sts × 30 rows per 4 in (10cm) over St st
Ball size: 142 yds (130m) per 1¾oz (50g) ball
Yarn specification: 57% fine merino wool, 33% microfiber, 10% cashmere

Rowan *RYC Natural Silk Aran*

A medium-weight silk-blend yarn

Recommended needle size: size 7 (4.5mm)
Gauge: 19 sts × 25 rows per 4 in (10cm) over St st
Ball size: 71 yds (65m) per 1¾oz (50g) ball
Yarn specification: 73% viscose, 15% silk, 12% linen

Rowan *Spray*

A super-bulky-weight wool yarn

Recommended needle size: size 15 (10mm)
Gauge: 9 sts × 11 rows per 4 in (10cm) over St st
Ball size: 88 yd (80m) per 3½ oz (100g) ball
Yarn specification: 100% merino wool

Rowan *Tapestry*

A lightweight wool-blend yarn

Recommended needle size: size 6 (4mm)
Gauge: 22 sts × 30 rows per 4 in (10cm) over St st
Ball size: 131 yds (120m) per 1¾oz (50g) ball
Yarn specification: 70% wool, 30% soya bean protein fiber

Yeoman *Cotton Cannele 4ply*

A fine-weight mercerized cotton yarn

Recommended needle size: size 2 (2.75mm)
Gauge: 33 sts × 44 rows per 4 in (10cm) over St st
Cone size: 930 yds (850m) per 8¾ oz (250g) cone
Yarn specification: 100% cotton

abbreviations

alt	alternate
beg	begin(ning)
cm	centimeter(s)
cn	cable needle
cont	continu(e)(ing)
dec	decreas(e)(ing)
garter st	garter stitch (k every row)
foll	follow(s)(ing)
g	gram(s)
in	inch(es)
inc	increas(e)(ing)
k	knit
m	meter(s)
M1	make one stitch by picking up horizontal loop before next stitch and working into back of it
mm	millimeter(s)
oz	ounce(s)
p	purl
patt	pattern
psso	pass slipped stitch over
rem	remain(ing)
rep	repeat
rev St st	reverse stockinette stitch (p all RS rows, k all WS rows)
RS	right side
sl	slip
st(s)	stitch(es)
St st	stockinette stitch (k all RS rows, p all WS rows)
tog	together
WS	wrong side
tbl	through back of loop(s)
yd(s)	yard(s)
yo	yarn over right needle to make a new st
*****	repeat instructions after * (or between *) as many times as instructed
******	work up to ** (or between **) as instructed

acknowledgments

My personal thanks and appreciation go to the exceptional people who have collaborated to create this book.

The team at Quadrille Publishing, especially Editorial Director, Jane O'Shea, my mentor, for her constant encouragement and style. Creative Director, Helen Lewis, for her tireless innovation on each new project. Lisa Pendreigh, my wonderful project manager for her rigorous support and inimitable professionalism.

It has been a privilege to have Katya de Grunwald photograph this book; her exceptional and distinctive work, together with stylist Beth Dadswell's unique and inspirational concepts have surpassed my wildest expectations. Thank you also to Anita Keeling our fabulous make-up artist and the stunning model Amy Browne at Premier Model Management.

My heartfelt thanks to Sally Lee, my brilliant project maker, for her constant support, enthusiasm, expertise, and friendship. And of course Eva Yates and Sally Harding for their inestimable and meticulous hard work in pattern checking.

Stephen Sheard of Coats Craft UK for consistently championing me and Kate Buller, brand manager of Rowan Yarns, and the team for their generosity and enthusiastic support. Also Tony Brooks of Yeoman Yarns for his invaluable assistance.

Finally, this book is dedicated to 'creatives' everywhere who continually excite with their passion for the hand made and who push the boundaries of craft by their enthusiasm and innovation. You are my constant source of inspiration.